Women Like Me

Journey Through the Eyes of Kenyan Women

Julie Fairhurst

Rock Star Publishing

Compiled by Julie Fairhurst
Copyright Julie Fairhurst 2023 – Rock Star Publishing
Paperback Edition: ISBN:978-1-990639-16-6
Interior & Cover Design by STOKE Publishing

Contents

Part Two
About Women Like Me

"There is no middle class in Africa.
There is poverty masked with graduation gowns and debts."

David Shamala

Introduction

Welcome, Dear Reader.

First, let me personally thank you for the purchase of this book. The proceeds directly go to support its Kenyan authors. By acquiring their work, you contribute to their families' well-being, ensuring food, clothing, and education for their children.

As you delve into the pages of "Women Like Me in Kenya," be aware that you're not merely embarking on their journey through their stories but also stepping into the vibrant, challenging, and inspiring lives of 21 extraordinary women.

Each word penned, each tale spun, stands as a testament to their strength, resilience, and spirit.

Their stories, each unique and powerful, are bound together by a shared goal: ***to earn a livelihood, to nourish their families, to clothe their children, and to bestow upon them the invaluable gift of education.***

Introduction

In the heart of Africa are the powerful beats of women's hearts. Telling the story of their nation with the spirit of their Kenya hearts. Their stories are tales of resilience, hard work, and determination.

Often overlooked, women are the lifeblood of Kenya, a testament to the strength and spirit of its country. It is these stories that "Women Like Me in Kenya" seeks to tell, shedding light on the lives that have long deserved to have their stories told.

Unsurprisingly, Kenyan women have long been pillars of their communities. They are the history, the champions of their culture, and the bearers of future generations. Their stories give us a unique view into Kenya. Through their eyes, we witness the monumental events and the daily intricacies that make up the Kenyan tapestry.

With "Women Like Me in Kenya," readers are invited to sit at these storytellers' feet, listen, learn, and most importantly, understand. Dive into these pages and emerge with a deeper appreciation for the land, the people, and the invincible spirit of Kenyan women.

These are not just stories; they are windows into the daily triumphs and trials faced by these women, the choices they've made, and the sacrifices they've borne. They write of Kenya, its rich tapestry of culture, tradition, and change, but they also write of universal themes - love, hardship, joy, and hope.

By choosing this book, you're not just gaining insight into the heart of Kenya through the eyes of these remarkable women; you're also supporting their noble endeavors. Every purchase is a pledge of solidarity, a gesture that says you recognize, honor, and uplift their journey.

May their stories inspire you, enlighten you, and remind you of the profound impact that the written word can have.

Introduction

Here's to the dreams, aspirations, and tenacity of the 21 women whose voices echo through these pages. And here's to you, dear reader, for joining them on this journey.

Welcome to a journey through Kenya – through the eyes of the strong women who define it.

Julie Fairhurst

Founder of Women Like Me

"Be very proud of your name and where you come from. It's so important. Say it loud and clear for everybody to hear."

Masai Ujiri

Part One
Journey Through the Eyes of Kenyan Women

Chapter 1
Water
The Gift of Life

"Thousands have lived without love, not one without water."
H. Auden

Our community has run out of water, which has brought many waterborne diseases. Due to this, people have tried as much to dig boreholes (wells), but this failed due to a lack of capital.

This has led many to develop different diseases like cholera and diarrhea. There was a time when society developed a project of building and creating water pipes to help us avoid having to fetch our water directly from ditches or holes.

In my area, there are still streams where water is fetched using guards or jugs, of which, when it rains, the water remains dirty throughout. We ought to get clean water because this is said to be life. When it's time for fetching water from said "good streams," they are still far away. This makes the distance tiresome for some of us. Many are unable to make that journey.

Other people have tried to dig these free open boreholes, and we, as women, see that this is dangerous to our children. This happened when they wanted water near their homes or within the compound, but then, due to lack of financial support, they never got the materials to finish the boreholes well. This is why they are dangerous. They are left unfinished.

The ropes made to fetch the water from the boreholes would sometimes break, making it difficult to fetch the dirty, soiled water from the holes.

There are areas where you can get water from a tap-made machine, but very few due to the large population. One would go a long way and have to wait a very long time to get the water from the tap.

Waterborne diseases have dropped because whenever one would get some small income in the form of money — this would go for fixing the water structure. But there is poor water structure in my area and illness is still happening.

As Women Like Me, we saw it better if we could bring water structures in our homes or even in our houses, that we may fetch water into them and put into two parts some water clearing tablets, sodium stones, and even water guards to keep safe drinking water. This would prevent some of the water-borne diseases.

Speaking on the use of these water guard medicines, we notice some people cannot use the drugs due to allergies. This creates a big problem for those people. We all need clean water to live healthy lives.

AGNESS NAMKURU

"In Kenya, you've got the great birds and monkeys leaping through the trees overhead. It's a chance to remember what the world is really like."

Joanna Lumley

Chapter 2
The Story About My Country
It's Not All Good

"The world is a dangerous place, not because of those who do evil,
but because of those who look on and do nothing."
Albert Einstein

In our country of Kenya, we have witnessed many crimes and groups who commit robbery. They also are killing people so that they don't have problems being caught.

In a short time, the people of Kenya have always witnessed hunger. We have locusts that always eat food in the garden. This makes it very difficult to grow food. So, many people, young and old, suffer a lot due to hunger!

Early death in our communities and country, of all ages, has led many children to become orphans. We thank our president because they are trying to fix this, but it is a struggle.

In some places in our country of Kenya, like Turkana, the lack of security is at a high rate, so we are praying for our president to help them and provide them with security.

In the year 2020, there was a big disease called coronavirus (COVID-19) that came from another country, and we didn't get the proper care, so many people died, and others were admitted to hospital (quarantine). Also, it led to more hunger, and some people died because of no food.

In our country, our girls have early pregnancy, and they get married very young. Because of this, life is very hard for our young girls. So, our president is fighting to get all the children an education. Education will help our nation's people improve in many areas of life.

We are strong in faith that soon our country will raise children in all education levels and get knowledge to support their communities and villages.

GMALDA WANZALA

"African women in general need to know that it's OK for them to be the way they are - to see the way they are as a strength and to be liberated from fear and from silence."

Wangari Maathai

Chapter 3
Weather In Kenya
Sunrises and Rain Storms

"Who cares about the clouds when we're together? Just sing a song
and bring the sunny weather."
Dale Evans

I want to talk about the weather in my country of Kenya. All January
we are receiving sun and all our country remains with more and more
hot days. If we receive wind, this means our weather is changing.

In April, we started to receive rain, and we started planting maize
and beans. But rain can come with a strong force, and we can get
meal that we plant or not. We never know for sure. At another time,
we don't know if we can get our meal on our land or not. This can be
very sad for us and hard on our people.

If rain begins to rain, well, September is the month we can harvest
our meal from the land with a lot of work. So, to get this meal, is not
easy. You can get another maize started,, but because we get no sun,
we don't know if it will come.

But I heard we have other people that are using powerlifting, but in our area, we don't have powerlifting. So, it is a struggle for our people to prepare the meal. We must do everything by our hands and our strong backs.

And when we started removing the meal from the land. Then the price of the meal came down. You cannot sell it to be able to change maize to money. We, the people of Western Kenya, are looking for another plan to help the community. We must all eat to survive.

Strong Women Like Me in Kenya, let us see what we can plant so it can help our community.

I am strong because my heart is strong. Hallelujah, Amen

CORINA WANGA

"The only man I envy is the man who has not yet been to Africa – for he has so much to look forward to."

Richard Mullin

Chapter 4
Not Enough Food
Western Kenya

"If you can't feed a hundred people, then just feed one."
Mother Teresa

I am Beldine Aoko, I come from Matura, Kenya. This is a small community found in Etenje. Sub-location, Mumias, sub-county in Kakamega County. This is in the western part of Kenya.

It's a small village, as indicated above, but the population is somehow higher than the village. Due to the increased population, people have been led to great famine, forcing some of the younger generation to steal.

Not enough land to plow or dig means not enough food for the families. Life has become so difficult that no one is gaining hope for tomorrow. This is a sad situation.

This has led to many deaths — Each and every one of the villagers owns and needs the same land. Oh my God! What a difficult life!

No total hope for tomorrow but I personally pray to God to give us a way forward. For our poor community to change for the better.

Young women are left widows so early that they fail to understand what life is. May the lord open the communities eye's to see what is to come.

The community ought to look forward so that their children may have some hope for the life of tomorrow.

BELDINE AOKO

"I never knew of a morning in Africa
when I woke up that I was not happy."

Ernest Hemingway

Chapter 5
Kenya
Our Leaders are Working to Help The People

"I got a taste when I was in Kenya a while ago of what medical care was in rural Africa. I was in a town of about 10,000 people, and a shipping container with a rusty microscope was their medical clinic."
Paul Allen

After five years, Kenyans elected leaders in our country, and all leaders were elected. All Kenyans came together as one family of peace, love, and unity in our villages and communities and all over to elect a leader who can lead well.

All Kenyans came together as one nation to support our nation with taxes. Everyone is supporting our nation by giving out taxes. Kenyans are coming together to have meetings to plan together how all of our citizens will come to be well.

In our nation, the language is Kiswahili_this is our national language. This language we are learning in schools. This is how we can communicate with everyone. (Swahili, also known by its local name Kiswahili, is a Bantu language spoken by the Swahili people, who are found primarily in Tanzania, Kenya, and Mozambique - Wikipedia)

Everyone has the freedom to stay anywhere he or she wants in our nation. Everyone has the freedom to go to any school he or she wants. Everyone has the freedom to build a house and the freedom to go to church. We are appreciative of this life, and we love this life in Kenya.

Our nation uses radio, television, phones, and magazines. Bad roads are breaking our communication; in other areas, we need power-lifting, and we don't have it. In other places, we have people staying in shacks with no lights.

In our nation, leaders have prepared markets for selling things. So, because of the preparation of the market, many villagers are starting businesses to sell things like oil, manure, and steel. This is a good plan for our Nation.

In our nation, we have a high population of people but not enough land. So, our leader has made plans to reduce the number of people. This plan is family planning. As Kenyans, we need to come together like one family, and all people should have only three children, not like the 20 children that we have going on today.

In our nation, people like to eat ugali only. So, people in Kenya are planting maize. Because if we eat ugali, we stay strong because we are doing the Lord's work, so they need to be strong, and our children are drinking porridge of flour; a child of two months has started eating ugali with green vegetables. (Ugali, also known as posho, sima, and other names, is a type of corn meal made from maize or corn flour - Wikipedia)

We thank God for the rain, Hallelujah!

In the sector of hospitals in Kenya, we have no medicines and don't have enough doctors. Our leaders are trying their best to ensure we have medicine in our hospitals, but it is not happening.

Money is a challenge to pay the doctors, but we have preparation on how we can get enough doctors and how they can receive payment. Our leader has prepared how we can get medicine into our country.

IRENE INDAKWA

"The drums of Africa still beat in my heart."

Mary Bethune

Chapter 6
My Village Called Buchiti
And the People Who Live There

"Our lives begin to end the day we become
silent about things that matter."
Martin Luther King, Jr

My village is called Buchiti, and it is where I got married. It is a small village where most of the people are poor. The market is far away from where I am living. Even the road is bad.

Education in our village has been very hard in the past years. The school has very little, and most schools in my village were poor in education. Only one school in my village was educated well and had many pupils pass the exam, but school fees were a problem, preventing some students from getting an education.

Many people have little gardens in my village, and people who have those gardens sell what they grow in that garden from far away. Where I got married, the garden was shared into small pieces for each of us. There were many of us.

Women Like Me

In my village, we have many problems with drugs and drinking. A lot of youth is engaged in drug abuse. Even little children went into drug abuse, and others left their jobs because of drugs.

Secondly is robbery. Most of the youth are engaging in robbery. They left school because of the robbery. Most are done during the night, and many things like cows, sheep, goats, and chickens are stolen.

And lastly, slaughter. Many people die because of the slaughter. They used many things like knives. So, there are some problems found in my village. But I pray to my God to change our village. I believe in my God, and like Women Like Me, to change our situation.

EVELYNE MULISI

"You can't hate the roots of a tree and not hate the tree. You can't hate Africa and not hate yourself."

Malcolm X

Chapter 7
Childless Women
By the Grace of God, Some of Us Have Children

"At the cry of a new born salt is being sprinkled
at the wound of a barren woman."
Peter Adejimi

In our village, we have many groups of women that are sitting together to share their lives in the village. But we have other women that teach you well or wrong. We have other women who don't have children and others that do have children.

You need to be careful when you sit with those who don't have children; be careful of anything you say to her because I learned that our sisters who don't have children have another kind of pain that is eating them.

So, think before you speak with them. Let your story give them joy, not make them remain in pain in their lives. And those women who have children love every woman that will come near to you, everyone has challenges. We have other people who don't respect women with no children.

Remember, it is by the grace of God that we have our children.

Let us encourage the women in our villages that every situation they are facing is for a short time, not all the years of their lives.

Thank you for reading and understanding.

ANGELINE KWAYU

"In Africa, you have space...
there is a profound sense of space here, space and sky."

Thabo Mbeki

Chapter 8
Men In My Community
Polygamy and Monogamy

"Nothing in this world was more difficult than love."
Gabriel García Márquez

Men in my community practice polygamy, and some of them practice monogamy. Men in our community are good to us because they marry wives, and God gives them families. Men in our community need love to have wives.

When a wife starts giving birth to children, the problem starts there because of the hardness that is happening in our marriage, but we still love them. When God gives children, many families separate because of the responsibility.

Many men in the community continue drinking alcohol. If someone goes home, they should not ask him anything if he has been drinking alcohol. To do so would cause problems. So, wives remain only in the houses.

So many women in my community run away because of their husbands drinking alcohol, and some go to Saudi to do some work there so that she can help her children with the provision of basic needs like clothes, food, and shelter.

Some children are living alone without their mothers. When the husband sees this, some will stay with their children, but others marry another wife and start living with this woman. The problem remains like the first problem for the children.

When that first wife comes back, they find that everything in the home compound has changed because of the second wife. She got a new wife and children, and when she sent money for school fees for the children, the children got no money, and they didn't even get to go to school.

So, here in Kenya, many wives are not in the house. They are doing house help in another Country.

So, as Pastors, if we get children like that, we take them back to school and speak with their teachers to help these children, but it becomes very hard for these children to go to school.

Another challenge in my community is that some people are living hard lives. Because life is not good, children don't have clothes because of poverty. Some people have jiggers because they cannot afford or get things like soap, blankets, and shoes. This life makes our community stay in the hard life. (Tungiasis is a painful skin infection caused by a flea called Tunga Penetrans/jiggers, which enters the epidermis of humans and animals. If untreated, it may result in bacterial infection, sepsis, necrosis, and disability. In Kenya, it is estimated that 4% of the population suffers from jigger infestation. http://www.jigger-ahadi.org/index.html)

We have hospitals in our community. We thank God. In the hospital, the problem is medicine. If you go to the hospital, you cannot get it. The only medicine available treats malaria, but if you have another sickness, you must go to another hospital far away from the community, which you need to pay for.

Without money, many people die, but others get healed through prayer and medicine.

EUNICE NERINA

"Africa is not a country, but it is a continent like none other. It has that which is elegantly vast or awfully little."

Douglas Wilder

Chapter 9
Challenges Faced In Kenya
May the Lord Help our Community

"The things you do for yourself are gone when you are gone, but the things you do for others remain as your legacy."
Kalu Ndukwe Kalu

Early marriage affects many people in Kenya. Most of our youth get married at a very early age. Others drop out of school because of these early marriages. This affects their education very much.

Circumcision affects many people negatively due to lack of proper training in the area. Many people bleed to the extent of dying because of a bad or unfair operation. This also leads to diseases like syphilis, gonorrhea, and other different diseases.

There are many children in our country who are not able to go to school because they can't afford school fees. This is when many children take on jobs for the family's basic needs. The young girls are labored out and don't go to school.

We have a lack of hospitals in Kenya. This leads to the loss of lives of many people due to lack of medicine. There are few hospitals, and most are in urban areas where people are struggling to get to the hospitals because they are so far away. At times, there are no doctors in the hospitals.

CHALLENGES

Examples of challenges in our small community are things like misunderstandings and too many arguments. Everybody claims to know what he or she does not know. This makes it impossible to help, guide, and control one another.

Some of the challenges are too many with alcohol and this even affects business women who are trying to succeed in getting their basic needs. It has made many young men and women get into drunkenness and forget their families. Young boys drop out of school because of drunkenness. Oh god, please help Matura.

In the village, there are elders, though, the challenges have made them to be silent as if they were not happening! As they keep arguing about who is to do what, seasons change, and things grow older in the Matura area. And all stays the same. Woe!

Some of the elders in my community migrated to another country (Uganda) due to the lack of land in the community. Others did it to escape providing for their families due to their difficult life.

Today, the young, married generation almost all get addicted to alcohol. The remaining percentage, I thank God, tries as much to seek the Lord, although in different denominations.

The young unmarried generation is mostly led to theft and alcohol. Only a few of them try to seek salvation.

May God help Kenya to gain the needed issues for our people to live a fair life.

ANN KWEYU

"I am not African because I was born in Africa but because Africa was born in me."

Kwame Nkrumah

Chapter 10
Kenya Tourist Attractions
I Invite You to Our Country

"Africa gives you the knowledge that man is a small creature, amongst other creatures, in a large landscape."
Doris Lessing

I am happy to be a Kenyan citizen by birth. I thank God for my marriage and the children given to me. Even though life was not better when I was born. I thank God nowadays for moving me step by step.

I keep on encouraging myself that to be a successful person, I must pass through challenges like in the bible. God tells the devil to go and destroy Ayub's belongings, including his wife and children. But when Ayub was tempted, he only asked God for help.

When I found myself in a difficult situation, I remembered that this is what makes me who I am.

In Kenya, there are major tourist attractions that include wildlife. Wild animals, birds, and natural vegetation attract many tourists to the game parks in our province. Many tourists visit Lake Nakuru so that they can see the flamingos found there. Women Like Me all over the world, I would like to invite you to our country.

Beautiful sites and features also attract tourists to the province. These include beautiful craters such as Menengai and Longonot. Lakes such as Barringo, Nakuru, and Naivasha. Rift Valley and its escarpments. The hot springs and stream jets at Lake Bogoria and Hells Gate.

Historical sites such as Kariandusi, Olorgesailie, Turkwel, Gorge, Hyrax Hill, and Fort Teman also attract tourists. The cultures of different communities in Rift Valley also attract many tourists. The way they dress, food, songs, dances, and other cultural activities are major tourist attractions in the Rift Valley Province, for example, the Maasai and Kalenjin Dances.

The warm weather in the province attracts many tourists from other countries. The tourists come mainly from cold countries.

Women Like Me, when you come, you will feel at home in our country because the people are welcoming and friendly.

Features such as Mt. Elgon and Kakamega forest also attract many tourists to the province. The sites I would like the Women Like Me to come and enjoy are the crying stone of Kakamega, and caves such as the Mungoma Caves and the Klebaye Falls—historical sites such as Nabongo Tombs and Chetambe Fort. I would like you to enjoy watching the Tsikuti dances, bullfighting, and cockfighting festivals where I stay.

JOSEPHINE AKINYI

"One of the great things about travel is that you find out how many good, kind people there are."

Edith Wharton

Chapter 11
The History Of Kisumu
My Story Living There

"Every sunset brings the promise of a new dawn."
Ralph Emerson

My name is Elizabeth Chiseka. I would like to share with you my history of living in Kisumu. I was uplifted in the county of Kisumu.

I moved to Kisumu in the year 2011, in the month of January, from Nairobi. My husband got a job in a rich man's house who promised to look after our children.

Everything started to change, and it was okay for a while. Meanwhile, I started a business, and our children went to school. I got the benefit of worshiping my God, and I thank my God for everything in my life.

The challenges I faced in Kisumu County started with my husband losing his job due to an accident, and my business dropped down.

That is when I knew the good of Kisumu County and the bad of it. My husband's teeth were no more, and it affected his life. I thank God because he removed my situation.

What hurt me in Kisumu County was that the rich man who had employed my husband chased us like his enemy, even though we lived with him like one family. It hurt me like a mother when I saw my family in trouble.

That is when I knew in Kisumu County, there was a separation of groups.

I tried to search for a bursary for my children, but I could not get someone to help me because I come from Kakamega County. Like a Kenyan, I got disturbed.

I thank God for removing me from that situation. I decided as a mother to go back home to Kakamega County with my family.

The people of Kisumu County search for the love of God because the grace of God will uplift you. To the one who will read this book, God bless you.

ELIZABETH CHISEKA

"You are not a country, Africa. You are a concept. You are not a concept, Africa. You are a glimpse of the infinite."

Ali Mazrui

Chapter 12
I Am A Kenyan
And a Women Like Me

"If you want to go fast, go alone. If you want to go far, go together."
African Proverb

I am a Kenyan. I live in the western part of Kenya. Although we have 47 counties, my county is Kakamega. I have various challenges that I want to share with you as Women Like Me. I see some of these challenges, I included them below.

Lack of treatment. This is when somebody is sick; he or she cannot get the proper treatment and eventually dies. There is no medicine in the hospital. That is another problem. We have a lack of clean water in certain areas. This causes typhoid fever in the area.

Early pregnancies are happening for those girls who are still learning. Many of them drop out of school. Another serious issue is that most of them turn to prostitution to satisfy their basic needs. This leads them to die early from HIV.

Although the Ministry of Education and the late Magoha had announced free education. Things are not this way. There is no free education in our country.

Another challenge is about worship. There have been many churches introduced to my country. There are some ministries that are true and some that are not true. This causes a lot of confusion to the members. At this moment, some churches are closed by the government.

Another challenge is that our country runs short of food, rain, etc. The cost of goods in shops is higher to buy. It makes it difficult for people to get food. Many of our people are jobless.

I thank Pastor Julie for your blessings. We appreciate you because you are a blessing to us. You have fed us, even dressed us. By our almighty God bless you all.

Lastly, I would like to show appreciation to our president because he has tried as he can to do what's right for human rights.

I am sure that he is going to continue to change our situation through God, I hope everything will be alright.

All of you Women Like Me please pray for my country. That God may meet and solve our problems.

May God bless you,

JESCA MBAYI

"In Africa, music is not an art form as much as it is
a means of communication."

Vernon Reid

Chapter 13
Emokua
Our Little Village in Western Kenya

"Tears shed for another person are not a sign of weakness.
They are a sign of a pure heart."
José N. Harris

I am a mother of four children living in a small village called Emokua. The village is located in the western part of Kenya, Kakamega County. Most of the villagers practice farming and small businesses in order to make their daily bread.

The lord is so productive for agriculture in the village. Sugar cane is the most cash crop planted in different parts of the area. The main problem affecting my area is that some villagers are unmotivated and not working at all. Our husbands are drunkards and are using prostitutes in most cases. Their support is very rare to their families.

About 90% of women are living without husbands. This results in a decrease in population. It is a laughing matter that "mamas" don't conceive because their husbands are drunkards and live far away from them.

In addition to this, most of the men in the community spend much time away from their families. They are also unable to educate their children due to the lack of school fees. Because of this situation, there is a high rate of theft in the area.

Another obvious problem is that the children who do not go to school have formed a group (gang) called the Forty-two Brothers which disturbs the villagers at night. The group walks around carrying sharp instruments like swords to kill people. This led to great problems in the village, including insecurity and displacement of others.

Another point I'd like to make is that some of them do not believe in God. They rely on idols and worship them, too. They practice witchcraft and believe in science. Others believe in ancestral spirits.

My prayer is that God will shape my village into a better one. I urge all Women Like Me in Kenya and all over the world to pray for my village, Emukoa. We need our husbands back from prostitute areas. We ought to bear children for the generation to come.

God Bless,

LILLIAN MUKONYI

"We are all children of Africa, and none of us is better or more important than the other. This is what Africa could say to the world: it could remind it what it is to be human."

Alexander McCall Smith

Chapter 14
Cattle Sleep In The House
So, They Don't Get Stolen

"There is a saying in Tibetan, 'Tragedy should be utilized as a source of strength.' No matter what sort of difficulties, how painful the experience is, if we lose our hope, that's our real disaster."
Dalai Lama XIV

I thank God because he made me to be a Kenyan. I am proud of our country. We have the freedom to worship.

The first challenge is the economy in our country. In our schools, we have to pay school fees. We have diseases like Malaria, which is at a high rate, and there is a lack of medicine in the hospitals.

We don't have food, and lack of money is a problem, so we stay in a life of struggling. We have death in our country. Many families lost their relatives through accidents and because of lack of food. And some marriages don't have peace.

In some places like Turkana, animals also die from lack of food or getting lost. When you walk anywhere, we have problems with robbers taking our cattle. This means everyone sleeps with their cattle in the house. Some people get killed over this.

We lack water, but sometimes we also have a lot of rain, making transporting things an even bigger problem. Some bridges are broken because of the flooding, and there is lots of damage to houses.

Early pregnancy in this country is at a high rate. Some boys are high and drunk. Some use miraa, or bang, so they don't have respect for their parents. Some become robbers and steal people's property.

Lack of jobs in our country. We have some well-educated people, but getting a job is a big problem. This leaves our children jobless and puts a lot of stress on the children.

So, I want to thank the almighty God for giving us the strength to continue to worship and believe in him, and we are still moving ahead with the word of God that says that whoever believes in God will stay in peace.

We need to believe in God the Father because he protects and fights for our lives up to the end.

JACKLYNE AKUMU

"Africa is one continent, one people and one nation."

Kwame Nkrumah

Chapter 15
Parents Are Afraid To Educate Their Children
They Fear Their Child will be Killed

"At what point do you give up - decide enough is enough?
There is only one answer really. Never."
Tabitha Suzuma

I am a woman of old age. I got married in 1940 in the village called Ebusikairs. This is in Kakamega County in the western part of Kenya.

I had a better and happier marriage when I had children. It was quite a good village where people associated with each other. Whenever anyone had an issue, we would come together to find a solution.

The village is rich in food; most people are hard-working, but a small portion are lazy. Their laziness has made people to be gossipers due to idol minds. Others have become robbers due to having a lack of basic needs. This forces them to take other people's property in order to survive.

In the village, some people are jealous. They don't like to see other people prosper. For example, when you educate a child to the university level or even to an institute or college, they ensure that the child is killed. Due to this, some people today are afraid to educate their children.

We have lots of witches in the village. Many people do not love God and avoid God. There is too much drug abuse, which has led many to poverty.

Many young people drop out of school because of drug addiction. Almost 75% of our children are illiterate. It is so sad that some people keep snakes, frogs, and mongoose in my village for witchcraft.

They take care of them like they are their own children. They are given bedding and fed and cleaned like human beings. You get a good parent feeding their gods and yet cannot afford to feed their own family! They spend more time with their gods than with their families.

I pray to God every night to help my area. We need pastors, prophets, and professors in my area. Whenever you share my story, please, I need your prayers. I appreciate Pastor Julie for your blessings. They make us happy and smart every now and then. You've dressed and even fed us.

May the living God of Isaac, Abram, and Jacob bless you even more.

Bye, God Bless,

MAGRET OTUBULA

"Never, never and never again shall it be that this beautiful land will again experience the oppression of one by another."

Nelson Mandela

Chapter 16
I Cry In A Silent Tone
When I See the Street Children of My Village

"Never lose faith in yourself, and never lose hope; remember, even
when this world throws its worst and then turns its back,
there is still always hope."
Pittacus Lore

Praise the name of the living God. I'm Janepher Makokha. If surely
there is no God, I could not be where I am and would have been
forgotten.

My life was hard, but because of the hand of Jehovah, I am eating. I
am talking, and I am walking well because of his power. Since I got
married, I saw many things to be hard, but God has never forsaken
me. Instead of looming down, God raised me up, so I thank the
almighty god.

My god should be so much respected because there was a day, I went
to visit my uncle in Bungoma where I met people who were passing
through a hard time and situation, but when I saw that, I realized that
God loves me and my problems are little or small.

I felt myself crying in a silent tone and started praying. In that country, there are also street children actually, and when you see them, you can start crying because they are sick. They don't have food. They are eating remains in the compost. They're not even in school. These children are stealing glue or borrowing from other people. They pick up the remains from the dustbins. They lack assistance in many things.

There are also big mountains in my country. Young farmers do their farming in small gardens. They plant onions and tomatoes, but the drought really brings them down, and this creates poverty in the country. However, there are also paper industries, but due to a lack of enough gardens, there are not enough trees to make the industry work.

Life has become that difficult due to lack of money. This may make many young children unlearned because of a lack of fees, school uniforms, and enough materials to maintain their learning.

On not going to school, many people are addicted to drugs, which spoils their lives. In addition to that, there are young people who take loans so that they can even purchase a motorbike for their or their basic needs achievement, but by bad luck, this spirit of road accidents has become so much that people lose their lives today.

This makes the young fear road work (boda boala), yet their loans must be paid. We pray for God to help and reduce the rate of road accidents.

JANEPHER MAKOKHA

"I believe there is no sickness of the heart too great it cannot be cured by a dose of Africa."

John Hemingway

Chapter 17
Kenya My Country
My Story

"Everything that is done in this world is done by hope."
Martin Luther

The road to independence in Kenya was not a smooth one. It involved serious commitment and struggle by Kenyans to liberate their country from colonialism. Through courage and love for their country, many Kenyans were prepared to risk their own lives for freedom. After independence, Kenyan leaders played a significant role in the development of the country.

Some of these leaders include the following.

- Mzee Jomo Kenyatta
- Daniel Toroitich Arap Moi
- Oginga Odinga
- Thomas Joseph Mboya
- Ronald Gideon Ngala
- Professor Wangari Maathai

Jomo Kenyatta

A young man named Jomo Kenyatta started an amazing political journey in 1924. He went on to become one of the most influential leaders in Africa. It all started when he joined the Kikuyu Central Association, a political group representing the Kikuyu people.

In 1945, a big moment happened that would change the course of history in Africa. The 5th Pan African Congress took place in Manchester, bringing together leaders from all around the continent. Among the attendees was a person who would play a crucial role in the fight for freedom in his native land.

This legendary man, who would later become known as the founding father of Kenya's independent nation, was Jomo Kenyatta. The Congress was a game-changer for him, and he made a game-changing decision here. He and fellow delegates vowed to go back home and fight for their country's independence. Talk about making a lasting impact!

THE CHALLENGES HE ENCOUNTERED

The Kenyan government faced opposition from the Kenya African Democratic Union, which wanted a federal system. There were also differences among the Kenya African National Union, leading to the formation of the Kenya People Union. The North-Eastern province was plagued by insecurity caused by armed bandits known as the Shifta.

In Africa, there was a time when most people didn't own any land. This was due to how the land was handled during the colonial era. This led to a lot of poverty and disease. There was not enough money to do important things like develop the country. There was also a lack of skilled workers because not many people were educated. The roads and communication were also not very good. Also, some people were assassinated for speaking out against the government. This caused a lot of people to lose trust in their leader. There were also some ethnic tensions as some groups felt like they weren't being included in the country's growth and progress.

DANIEL TOROITIC ARAP MOI

Moi was elected as the member of Legco for Rift Valley in a by-election on October 14, 1945, after the previous member. He was also part of an African delegation to the first Lancaster House Conference, which focused on constitutional changes and led to Kenya's independence. In 1961, he was elected to the Legislative Council for Baringo and appointed Parliamentary Secretary for Education.

When we see here, we see that Kenyatta, as the past president of Kenya, gave the leadership to Moi because he was already dying. Kenyatta did good work and good arrangement of things in our nation. It means we must do all of our work well, without confusion. It means we must do our work well and arrange it accordingly because there is someone who is going to hand it over to him or her.

Women Like Me, let us plan good things like this leadership done, and we shall be blessed. Moi was a good leader in schools because he was the one who started 8.4.4 education. This means that each kid gets eight years in primary school, four years in secondary school, and four years in a university or college. We appreciate President Moi for it because that is the time people started to expand their minds with education. Many poor people struggle to get to school because of school fear, but good thing that President Moi was giving us milk every week in class. We appreciate everything here in Kenya. We need to be strong with a lot of faith, like our leaders. We need to find how we can get moving in everything without worrying about what is going on.

THE CHALLENGES HE ENCOUNTERED

There was a failed attempt to take down the government by a group of young Air Force members on August 1, 1982. A senior private, Hezekiah Babalah Ochuka, led this.

Pressure on President Moi's government to start allowing multiple political parties. There were ethnic clashes in parts of the country, including Mount Elgon, the Rift Valley, and the coast. There was a lot of damage and deaths. Corruption within the government, too, was happening. Officials were taking public land and misusing public funds. There were natural disasters happening and a lack of water.

MWAI KIBAKI

Did you know that Mwai Kibaki was the president of Kenya from December 2002 to April 2013? Before that, he was the 4th vice president from 1978 to 1988 under President Daniel.

He was one of the most long-lasting politicians in Kenyan history.

It is my opinion that Moi was a president who has done more for our nation because he is the one who made it possible for Kenyans to receive free education in primary school and high school.

But we gave out only lunch levee, and he used his knowledge to remember youth projects. He gave Kenyan youth to borrow a motorbike so that they could care for their families because we don't have any factories. But we thank him for the good work that he has done to help the poor people whose children went to school.

The youth who were poor learned how to drive a motorbike, and the price was not too high. Nowadays, the price of a meal, transport, school, and lunch levee is high, and everything is high, and life is becoming harder and harder.

THE ACHIEVEMENTS HE MADE

One of his projects was promoting agro-based industries and increasing agricultural exports. He also gave Kenya a new constitution. After Kenya gained independence in 1963, he won big at the KANU. The administration introduced free basic education and revamped hospitals.

He was honored for his efforts to promote harmony, understanding, and cooperation among different groups of people. His presidency between 2003-2012 was notable for several key achievements. I have a deep respect for him.

Thank you so much, Mwai Kibaki, for your family's struggle for the Kenyan's lives. We appreciate you; God bless your family.

During his time as our President, Kibaki faced lots of challenges in the country' including outbreaks of diseases like coronavirus and flooding. Lack of food for some people, rural-urban migrations, student dropouts, breakdown of markets and business. Lack of rainfall in some continents, and no greens. Death of animals and some people due to dehydration and many other challenges.

You have done more to our nation to help Kenyans. We appreciate you for the good work you have done for us. To care for people all these years is not easy. Because God has directed you in all these years, be blessed.

WILLIAM SAMOI RUTO

From 2013-2022, he was the vice president under President Uhuru Kenyatta. In September of 2022, he became the 5th president of Kenya. He's a strong man of God, full of confidence and faith.

Our president, William Samoei Ruto, cares about Kenyans' well-being. He has been working tirelessly to make things a bit easier for us, especially now that the prices of everything have been skyrocketing.

He is looking for solutions to keep Kenyans afloat. One of his top priorities is securing enough maize to feed everyone. He is also teaching us valuable lessons on water conservation and farming techniques so that we can grow more crops like corn, cassava, and potatoes, which will help us fight hunger and save many lives.

Let's work together to make our country a better place!

He announced the price of fertilizer will drop, which is good! But he's also dealing with some tough problems—people dying from hunger and thirst and the growth of slums. Plus, there's the issue of rural-urban migration and the lack of food and water in certain parts of the country.

We have some very caring religious leaders and a president who are working really hard to help the people in need in our community. Unfortunately, there's a shortage of food, clothes, and clean water, and the cost of living is very high.

I am a pastor here in Kenya, and I thank the mighty God for being in a Strong Women Like Me in Kenya. In my country, there are many interesting things that I would like to share with all the members of the group.

In Kenya, you would love it and enjoy the food. In Kenya, we have dairy keeping on some continents. We have the domestic keeping of animals. Our domestic animals include chickens, cows, dogs, sheep and goats.

When you come to our country, you will enjoy world life, museums, snake parks, lakes, big rivers, salty water lakes, and many others. Welcome to Kenya, and you could even see the crying stone in Nakuru. Welcome to Kakamega Forest.

We love our president in our country. God bless you, the man of God. We are looking for peace, love, and unity in our Nation, be blessed.

OUR COMMUNITY AND VILLAGES

Community in our country we are doing well. We thank God for the creation of this world. We love our country, Western Kenya.

In our community, we have leadership that is leading us, and we appreciate our country leaders for taking care of us to ensure everyone has peace.

We have our community leader who has elected ten people that are not sleeping at all at night because it is their duty to watch the area to make sure there are no robbers coming into our compound to steal things and kill our people.

Us Strong Women in Kenya say, "God bless our leaders." These people are doing the work, and no one is paying them. We are praying for God to protect them.

In our community, we love to keep cattle like cows, sheep, and goats. We have people moving all night to make sure our community is well. But we have robbers in the night that some to steal our cows and properties.

A SOLUTION

Though there are robbers within the community, there are enough patrols that some community members are not troubled.

EDUCATION

We thank God for the schools built within the community. This makes most of our children to be busy and learning. Even though we've got some challenges in schooling, i.e. (lunch allowance problems due to lack of jobs for parents.) Challenge two is the lack of school fees, causing some pupils to drop out of school, leading to drunkenness and robbery. Others use their leisure time in drug abuse.

Another great challenge is that others learn up to high school, but after that, they run into loss of jobs — This means that their education was meaningless to their lives. Others could never manage to join universities due to lack of money.

As a solution to this, we pray to God to help open financial doors so that we may get some materials to open even a single project to keep our children busy. If we could get carpentry materials, salon materials, etc., we think this may help a lot in our community.

We pray for them, we guide them, we counsel them, and more so, we may encourage them that one day, one time, the Lord will reach their cry.

I would also like to address little girls in my community. This has been a bigger challenge. Some people misuse them. Most of our girls suffer after reaching the puberty period. They lack sanitary pads, others drop out of school due to lack of school uniforms, which leads to early pregnancies, and some even drop out of school due to lack of food at home.

In my community, orphan pupils sometimes don't report to school due to a lack of stationery. They have no one to provide for them. One would only be lucky to meet a good Samaritan for support. Children such as these suffer so much because even having shelter becomes a problem for those who don't have close relatives. Some of them stay in very filthy streets, which causes them to be very weak and sickly.

As Strong Women Like Me, we pray for an orphanage to be funded in our community to protect and care for such children. Such children are our hope for tomorrow. They need to be shown love, they need to be protected, they need to be educated, and they need better shelter and clothing as well.

We have enough courage and are filled to the brim full of faith that this will be fulfilled by the will of our God.

WIDOWS AND WIDOWERS

In my community, we've got widows — a total of widows aged 75 years and above. They struggle much with life due to the older ages and have no help. So, they need some help because they stay lonely in their hutches.

We love them, but now we have nothing to give to them. In such cases, they go without food and have no bedding or even good clothing, but this has become a history of our lives. Seeing them is like a dream to many, and no one cares. Be they sick, be they in any need, only God knows.

Others live in the darkness without light. They go without shoes. This makes them develop foot diseases and even jiggers on their legs! They go to bed very early, without bathing due to lack of soap, and some of them due to the fear of water to their old skin. We may sometimes find them sleeping outside the hutch due to a lack of strength — this comes from no food or energizing snacks.

As Women Like Me, we ought to get some pairs of rubber shoes to protect them from jiggers. And even if we could get a way of building them good shelters and feeding them, this could greatly help the widows. They should at least get some clothing to prevent cold and some diseases caused by coldness, sweaters, blankets, etc.

They should be protected because their ages are too old. We have another president announced. If they have children to care for them with small money that our country is giving them, but we have others are getting that small money to help them, but others are not getting that money or another their children are going to take that money, and they are not giving to them. We need to reach people like this. These people are God's image.

PASTOR PAULINE AWINO ATITWAW

"The eye never forgets what the heart has seen."

African Proverb

Chapter 18
Men In Kenya
Holding onto Their Stress

"Instead of worrying about what you cannot control, shift your
energy to what you can create."
Roy T. Bennett

We have marriages in our County. People are marrying women. But
we hear another story: people want to marry man-to-man or wife-to-
wife in our country, as they do in other countries. I thank our country's leaders for carefully considering this situation. They came
together and decided this country was not ready for this, so we
continued to marry men and women. We appreciate our leaders who
are careful with every word in our country to ensure it is good or bad.
God bless our leader in this country.

Those who are getting married thank God because we live the life
written in the Bible. We thank God because of our relationships in
our marriages. We have children that God has given to us in our
households. But we have challenges in our house—all women in our
country. When women started to produce children, the problem
started there.

The men become drunks, and they use too much alcohol. The children remain with their mothers only. Those mothers are jobless, and children want to eat and go to school, but the mother has nothing to help them. When you ask their father, they say they don't have jobs, so they are using alcohol to remove stress.

So, women are struggling with their children to get school fees and food, which makes marriage and mothers run and look for jobs to help their children.

Many women are not in marriages. They are outside our country looking for the money to help their families.

But the men are staying at home waiting for what the wife was out getting her children, which is very painful for the ladies in our county. And women are not enjoying their marriages. Their marriage changed to be painful and sad in life. Because children miss their mothers when they grow up. The wives were missing their husbands, and the children were missing their mothers.

Are the ladies who will go to find out how she can build the houses at home? It is the lady who looks out for how people are going to eat. It is the ladies who know how their children will be treated. So Kenyan women are very strong in all!

We see if our nation can remember people in villages to get companies near them so they can rest. But if they cannot help them, how can they get jobs in the villages in the coming years? You will not get ladies in their marriages. All ladies are going to find house-girl jobs.

But let us come together like women to get what we can to care for our family as a family.

God Bless all, Amen.

JULIET OUTA

"You cannot leave Africa, Africa said. It is always with you, there inside your head. Our rivers run in currents in the swirl of your thumbprints; our drumbeats counting out your pulse; our coastline the silhouette of your soul."

Bridget Dore

Chapter 19
My Story
The Roads of My Community

"You have power over your mind - not outside events. Realize this,
and you will find strength."
Marcus Aurelius

We thank God because of transportation in our community. We have roads that are not very good, but I thank those people who are helping our community get good roads.

What is challenging us is that we have a lot of accidents on the road because people are drinking alcohol before they go traveling. People are not careful on the roads because other drivers do not use road signs, and others are careless.

We Kenyans need to learn road signs before we go to the road because the roads are finishing our people, our children. Like our school bus, check it before you go with it anywhere.

To all Kenyans, let us love our people drivers. We love all of you because you are carrying our life in the vehicle. Please be careful with your life and your own life.

We are praying for you all and telling our inside man that everybody will now read this message and give it out to everyone.

Be blessed.

MONICA KHAYASI

"To get lost is to learn the way."

African Saying

Chapter 20
My Village In Kenya
Where People Live a Hard Life

"It's not the load that breaks you down, it's the way you carry it."
Lou Holtz

I come from a small village by the name of Lukala, where people live a very hard life due to poverty. In my area, we have great problems with water, food, sources of light, lack of education, and lack of shelter.

In my village, there is a lack of clean water. Many people die from the water. We have dirty water, which causes some diseases. Some diseases like water borne diseases, malaria, bilharzia, cholera, and typhoid fever lead to the deaths of many people. Even animals die due to thirst.

The issue of having no clean water forces others to drink from bore-holes and streams, which is very dangerous to human beings. We pray to God to open doors for us to get clean water.

We have a shortage of food in our village, which causes some people to die of starvation and hunger. In our village, there is a lack of land to plow, and even for those who have smaller portions of land, there is a lack of fertilizer. This creates a lack of food in a larger portion. I believe that one day, God will greatly change my area.

The source of light is a problem. There is not enough electricity. This means people become victims of theft in the night. It even causes accidents at times. Without light, the wild animals get an advantage in hunting. Destroying humans, things, and property.

Lack of education has caused a great problem in our village, where we have idolatry. In some areas schools are quite far away, in my village we have only one school that is nearby.

May God help my area and give a way forward to find more schools.

PATRICIA FAITH

"Only the disciplined ones in life are free. If you are undisciplined, you are a slave to your moods and your passions."

Eliud Kipchoge

Chapter 21
Churches In Kenya
Many Denominations

"Africa has her mysteries, and even a wise man cannot understand them. But a wise man respects them."
Miriam Makeba

My name is Rose John, and I am an over-aged woman in the community, being a Christian. But in the years I've lived, I realized that there are too many churches of different denominations in my community.

This is good, and it means that most of the community members are Christian, too. There are Islamic sessions. They believe in and worship God, too.

The churches/buildings are so many that one only chooses where he/he fits. I thank God because of this. When I once was saved and got to know my God. I made a choice in my heart, and this is where I am today.

Women Like Me

The denominations and churches are many, but there are challenges, too. People believe in different beliefs, but I believe in my true God, who made/created the universe.

Today, other churches are confused, which has caused many to get into a fall. Other churches are not understandable, others are normal, and others are unknown.

In different types of worship, but all in all, they are churches.

God-fearing churches and others, or may we say "Satan" fearing churches. They don't worship the true God like today in Kenya. There are so many issues brought by the churches: confusions are many, leaders too many. Some of the pastors are after money. They have made the church a business place.

Woe unto the non-God-fearing churches. Today, you may get people killed in churches. Oh My God! This is a great problem and challenge in the Lord's ministries.

The many churches had brought less peace to the families. There are other churches that have changed the word of God. They do things the opposite way. This is a challenge to the community and even Kenya as a whole.

It is difficult to understand which church is which and which church is right. But we pray to God to reveal the true churches so that Kenya may get back to peace.

If I may address and tell you about my church, we love and serve God, and today, in our churches, you find more women than men. We don't have any reason for this, but you ought to know.

The population is growing higher and higher, and I came to realize that wherever there are instruments in the church, there will be a younger generation attending in good numbers. This means we, as Women Like Me, should do something that inner causes. We may redeem our young boys', and girls' lives for a better tomorrow, better servants, and better parents by attending regularly.

We sat down and looked at this, and if we could get more instruments, then we would gain or have some hope for the church to come.

Remember, a church is said to be oneself, so let's keep God's churches in us, Women Like Me; without looking backward, we should maintain and keep the faith that even if Christ came today, we will be found ready and sanctified.

Women would always go to their knees to seek their God or cry for their children. This will make a good church for tomorrow. May the Lord help my community. We fail to understand how to help this situation.

We pray to God in times to come. As we continue cooperating, we ought to build permanent, strong, and safe boreholes and, if possible, build and install the pipes that lead from the stream so that our community will be safe.

We pray to God to help us reach the goal. I personally am over-aged. Due to the distance, I cannot make the trip needed to get to the stream. I hope we will be ok if we all put our minds together.

ROSE JOHN

"Why is it you can never hope to describe the emotion Africa creates? You are lifted. Out of whatever pit, unbound from whatever tie, released from whatever fear. You are lifted and you see it all from above."

Francesca Marcian

Chapter 22
My Story About Nairobi
Our Capital City of Kenya

"What you do makes a difference, and you have to decide what kind
of difference you want to make."
Jane Goodall

Nairobi is the capital city of Kenya. It is more interesting compared to
other countries in Kenya. Many people move from rural areas to
Nairobi to search for job opportunities because of their poverty. In
Nairobi, we have many companies and industries, such as Jud Kali
Industry.

In addition, we have many people living there, which leads to high
population pressure in the city. Due to the high population, many
people lack a place to stay, which leads them to live in the slums
because they lack capital or money to afford houses. Many people
have established trading activities so that they can get their living
standards.

Most of the population are youth who have moved from rural to
urban, searching for job opportunities. However, after reaching
Nairobi, they have turned to robbery and forcing people to give them

their property or take their lives because they are refusing to give it to them.

The lack of job opportunities has increased due to the high population in the city. Whereby there are few jobs compared to how many people need employment.

Traffic jams. Many people have their cars or motorbikes, which force people's movement and properties to be very slow and, in some situations, cause traffic jams.

When the vehicles move, they emit dust particles and gases, which cause erosion of iron sheet and produces acid rain due to damage to the ozone layer by the chemicals and gases.

Nairobi is a good city because we have people practicing different businesses. People are enjoying life. The problem is we have a lack of meals, and we have many stray children who are sleeping in the dams. Let us pray for our nation.

ROSE JUMA

"It's really beautiful. It feels like God visits everywhere
else but lives in Africa."

Will Smith

Chapter 23
About My Country
The Good and The Bad

"Cry. Forgive. Learn. Move on.
Let your tears water the seeds of your future happiness."
Steve Maraboli

The high cost of living in Kenya has caused many people of Kenya to have a bad life. This leads to the prices of food increasing, increasing daily. For example, for one tin of maize food, one day it will be 250 shillings, and the next day it will be 300 shillings.

The land shortage had led to a hard life for the people of Kenya. We have more families but with a small piece of land. Shortage of land leads to shortage of food because there is no land for plantation. There is the poor business in Kenya and the death of lots of people.

The increase in population is another big challenge for the people of Kenya. In that high percentage of people live in countries because of the lack of land. The increase in population in Kenya has also led to a lack of job opportunities and job security.

Drug abuse has brought more harm to our community, more so to the youth. The young generation has become more addicted to drugs, which affects their lives. Drugs like bang, cocaine, and others like changes have caused young people to have bad lives.

The lack of jobs in youth has brought even more harm to Kenya. Many youths become thieves because they lack money. Some drop out of school and start doing bad things.

My name is Ruth Maende. I was born in 1998. My life was good and bad. We were born with four children. My father was very stubborn, but my mother did not give up.

We went to my grandmother's place. We grew up there and went to school there. We went on with life. My mother went to search for a job in Nairobi. My mother was sending money to my Grandmother, and we used it.

I went to school until the form and fees were no more. I went to search for a job of being a house girl. I got pregnant when I was still young. That's when I knew I had to move on with my life. I got married and moved on with my life.

RUTH JUMA

"We are not human beings having a spiritual experience. We are spiritual beings having a human experience."

Pierre Teilhard de Chardin

Chapter 24
Drought In Kenya
Loss of Water, Shortage of Food

"People must feel that the natural world is important and valuable
and beautiful and wonderful and an amazement and a pleasure."
David Attenborough

Drought has caused many challenges in our country. It had caused
both domestic and wild animals' loss of life and death. Loss of water
and shortage of food. Lots of young children drop out of school due to
a lack of food and school lunches. It forced them to go and find jobs
in order for them to satisfy their spirit of adventure.

Drought has caused many young girls to have early pregnancies and
early marriages. For example, it has caused a high cost of living in
Turkana. Drought has caused less farming altitudes, i.e., the disap-
pearance of plants and the death of domestic animals. This has led
Turkana to poverty.

We are asking God to help Turkana County. In Turkana, people eat
some roots of trees and wild fruits, lack enough water, and have hutch
houses. They are staying without clothes, staying without knowing
what they can do to help themselves. We are praying for Women

Like Me in the world that one day, we can go there in order to see them.

Some of the plants in Turkana are wilted, leaving the soil barren. This causes soil erosion, meaning the soil has lost its nutrients. In Turkana and other places in Kenya, we are experiencing low standards of living due to the lack of basic needs.

The wise young people have learned from their parent's difficulties and pray that the back life should no longer be to their portion. They are living to make changes in their community.

This has at least given us some hope for tomorrow. But the fact remains that our small community is highly populated! They intend to change the alcoholic businesses to other more beneficial businesses in the community. The drunkenness may at least stop or reduce for the young people moving to be able to look forward.

As Women Like Me, let's join hands together and support the young generation to fulfill their vision, for they are our children, our sons and daughters, and they may change tomorrow, too.

SWIZEX WASONGA

"I hope you have an experience that alters the course of your life because, after Africa, nothing has ever been the same."

Suzanne Evans

Chapter 25
Rain In Our Community
Malaria

"Courage is the most important of all the virtues because, without courage, you can't practice any other virtue consistently."
Maya Angelou

My name is Veronica. I live in Kakamega. It always rains from morning to evening, making people suffer a lot. Because we have people that don't have good houses, they stay in a hutch.

When rain falls, a lot of people get Malaria because of rain that is raining in their houses. A lot of people don't have mosquito nets, but I thank God that people are giving nets to our country.

And we love rain, because of the rain we get many greens in the garden. The problem is that it causes some people to catch Malaria and causes problems with our homes. Some people lose their houses and cattle, so they no longer have a home to stay in.

When the rain comes with so much force, it carries away our houses and everything in our houses—a lack of food. Even if we had planted crops, no profit, or no food because of the floods, big rain destroyed all the food. Some families stay in the schools, so they need help with shelter and clothes, and we have no water we can use in our homes because water is not clean for us.

In Kakamega, we have received rain, and rain is its blessing. We are looking to get tanks so we can save water when it rains, and when the time of the sun comes, we can use that water, us, the group of Strong Women Like Me in Kenya.

Be blessed.

VERONICA MUTAYI

"Be the change that you wish to see in the world."

Mahatma Gandhi

Part Two
About Women Like Me

Chapter 26
Women Like Me Community
Join The Movement

The power of women's stories lies in their ability to inspire, challenge, educate, and connect. They are both a reflection of individual experiences and a testament to collective strength. In sharing and honoring women's stories, we can recognize the contributions, challenges, and diversity of women's lives.

Empowerment Through Unity - One voice can make a sound, but a chorus can shake the earth. "Women Like Me" is more than just a movement; it's a collective voice of women from different walks of life coming together to make meaningful changes in society. By joining, you amplify that voice and make it resonate even louder.

Shared Experiences - No matter our backgrounds, women around the world face similar challenges. By joining this movement, you get access to a wealth of shared experiences and insights that can inspire and guide you in your personal journey.

A Safe and Supportive Space - The "Women Like Me" movement offers a platform where your voice is not just heard but celebrated. It's a space where you can express yourself without fear of judgment and where your experiences are validated.

Opportunities for Growth - Beyond sharing stories, this movement provides personal and professional growth opportunities. Members can access resources to help them thrive in their chosen paths through networking, workshops, mentorship programs, and more.

Making a Difference - The stories in the "Women Like Me book series" aren't just narratives; they serve a larger purpose. By supporting this movement, you directly contribute to empowering women to care for their families.

Celebrate Womanhood - At its core, the "Women Like Me" movement is a celebration of being a woman. It's an embrace of our strengths, vulnerabilities, stories, and potential.

In essence, joining the "Women Like Me" movement is more than just aligning with a cause; it's a declaration. It says you believe in the power of women, in shared stories, and in a future where every woman has the opportunity to shine. Will you lend your voice, your strength, and your passion to this vibrant tapestry of womanhood?

Join Us Here:

https://www.facebook.com/groups/879482909307802

"How wonderful it is that nobody need wait a single moment before starting to improve the world."

Anne Frank

Chapter 27
Women Like Me Book Series

Everyone has a story. And oftentimes, those stories can be powerful things that help us learn and grow. But for some people, their stories can be a source of pain. They may feel like they can't escape their past or that their story is holding them back from living their best lives.

If you're one of those people, know that you're not alone. And more importantly, know that there is hope. There are ways to turn your personal story into something positive and to find healing from the past.

One way is to share your story with others. This can be incredibly cathartic, and it can also help others who have been through similar experiences. you process your feelings and work through any trauma you may be carrying around. And finally, don't forget that your story doesn't define you. You are more than your history. You are more than your pain. You are more than your mistakes. You are more than your story. You are strong, you are brave, and you are enough. So don't let your story hold you back.

Writing about your past can be very beneficial, both emotionally and psychologically. You can increase your feelings of well-being and even improve your physical health. When you write about your past experiences, you relive them in your mind. This can help you to process difficult or traumatic events, and it can also provide you with some closure.

Additionally, writing about your past can help you to understand yourself better and work through any unresolved issues. It can also allow you to see yourself in a new light, which can be both healing and empowering. In addition to helping you emotionally, writing about your past can also be beneficial physically. Studies have shown that expressive writing can help to reduce stress, anxiety, and depression. It can also help to improve your immune system function and promote a sense of calm. So, if you're feeling stressed out or overwhelmed, consider picking up a pen and starting to write.

We only have one shot at this life, and it's our only shot. There are no do overs. There are no second chances. So, we better make the most of it. We only have this moment right here, right now, and it's the only moment that matters. We only have so much time on this planet and must spend it wisely. We only have so much energy and want to spend it on things that bring us joy. We only have so much love to give and want to give it to people who appreciate it.

A story is a powerful thing. It can draw you in, take you on a journey, and leave you with a lasting impression. That's why I love listening to other people's stories. Everyone has a story to tell, and I'm always eager to hear a new one.

Visit the Women Like Me Stories website at www.womelikemestories.com and get in touch. The world will be waiting.

Women Like Me Stories

https://womenlikemestories.com/tell-your-story/

We need women at all levels, including the top, to change the dynamic, reshape the conversation, to make sure women's voices are heard and heeded, not overlooked and ignored."

Sheryl Sandberg

Julie Fairhurst

Julie Fairhurst is the Founder of the Women Like Me Book Program. She is also a Certified Master Persuader, Sales Strategies, and Storyteller Coach. She started the Women Like Me Project to help women tell their stories. She helps her clients to share their message with the world through her unique storytelling programs. Julie has published 24 books and over 150 published authors to her credit.

Sales and marketing expert Julie helps women entrepreneurs build their influence and authority with their clients and customers so they can increase their revenue and profits. With a certification in persuasion and over 30 years of sales and marketing experience, Julie is an expert at understanding human behavior and what triggers people to make a purchase. She helps her clients develop marketing strategies that appeal to their target audience and provides coaching on how to close the sale.

In addition, she teaches her clients how to use the power of storytelling to engage and connect with their customers. As a result, they are able to build trust and credibility, which leads to more sales and higher conversion rates.

Julie is also a sought-after speaker, trainer, and prevention educator. She has been delivering empowering workshops to adolescents and adults on safety issues. She has presented to organizations such as the Vancouver Police Department, Justice Institute, University of British Columbia, and Capilano College. Behavioral Society of British

Columbia, Surrey Memorial Hospital. Teachers Association of North Vancouver, and Shine Live, as well as appearing on television and in video.

When Julie was young, her home life was chaotic and tumultuous. Her parents were constantly fighting, and she felt unsafe and unloved. As a result, she developed some bad habits and made some poor decisions. As a teenager, she was headed down the wrong path, and it seemed like there was no hope for her.

But, somewhere deep inside, that little girl inside her showed up and reminded her that she wanted better for herself and her kids. Julie had no support from anyone, not a soul. She had to do it all on her own. She had no help from anyone, not a single person. She had to do everything by herself.

It's not easy to change your life. In fact, it can be downright difficult. But it's also necessary if you want to move forward. Sometimes, you must take a step backward before going forward. And that's what happened to Julie.

Julie is a woman who has achieved great success in her life despite facing many obstacles. She is a great example of someone who did not let anything stand in her way. Despite these challenges, she never gave up. She went back to school and finished her education. She built an outstanding career in sales, marketing, and promotion. She won the company's top awards and was the first woman to achieve top salesperson year after year in a male-dominated industry. She was a sales manager for some of the country's most prestigious developers. She is an inspiration to everyone who knows her. She is proof that anything is possible with hard work and dedication.

Many people say that you should never look back, but Julie does. Why? Because she wants to remember the journey that brought her to where she is today. And today, her life is very different.

Then, in 2019, Julie's beautiful 24-year-old niece died from a drug overdose on the streets of Vancouver, Canada. And that was the day she said enough! Her niece's death indirectly resulted from the generational beliefs and abuse that some of her siblings continue with their destructive lifestyles. So, when Julie says, "Enough is enough," she means it! Unfortunately, her story isn't unique.

When we don't face our issues, we pass on dysfunctional behaviors to future generations. This is what happened to my young niece. This is why I started the Women Like Me organization. When children grow up in toxic environments, they often develop behavioral issues that follow them into adulthood. This can lead to serious problems in their relationships, careers, and mental health. My young niece was a victim of this.

Everyone has a story, and everyone's story matters. No matter what you've been through, you can improve your life. It's not always easy, but with determination and perseverance, anything is possible.

The first step is to believe in yourself. You have the power to create whatever future you want for yourself. The next step is to take action. You can't just sit and wait for good things to happen. You have to go out and make them happen. And finally, you have to persevere. There will be setbacks along the way, but that's no reason to give up. Keep going, and never give up on your dreams.

If you're willing to put in the work, you can change your life for the better. You have the power to do so. You just have to believe in yourself and take the steps to make it happen. So don't give up on yourself - you're capable of much more than you think. And when you're ready to get started, I'm here to help.

HERE IS HOW YOU CAN CONNECT WITH JULIE

Email: julie@changeyourpath.ca

Women Like Me Stories

www.womenlikemestories.com

Julie Fairhurst Academy

www.juliefairhurst.com

SOCIAL MEDIA

YouTube – Julie Fairhurst Women Like Me Stores and in Business

https://www.youtube.com/channel/
UChFnLgiUC9mWnvp7jikKBw

Women Like Me on Facebook

https://www.facebook.com/StoryCoachJulieFairhurst

Julie Fairhurst Academy on Facebook

https://www.facebook.com/juliefairhurstcoaching

LinkedIn - Julie Fairhurst Certified Master Persuader

https://www.linkedin.com/in/salesstrategistjuliefairhurst/

Instagram – Women Like Me Stories

https://www.instagram.com/certified_master_persuader/

TikTok – Sales Strategist

https://www.tiktok.com/@juliethesalesstrategist

Read More From Julie Fairhurst

Books are available on Amazon or the Women Like Me Stories website.

Sales and Personal Growth

Transferring Enthusiasm - The Sales Book For Your Business Growth

Positivity Makes All The Difference

Agent Etiquette – 14 Things You Didn't Learn in Real Estate School

7 Keys to Success – How to Become A Real Estate Badass

30 Days to Real Estate Action – Real Strategies & Real Connections

Why Agents Quit The Business

Women Like Me Book Series

Women Like Me – A Celebration of Courage and Triumphs

Women Like Me – Stories of Resilience and Courage

Women Like Me – A Tribute to the Brave and Wise

Women Like Me – Breaking Through the Silence

Women Like Me – From Loss to Living

Women Like Me – Healing and Acceptance

Women Like Me – Strong Women in Kenya

Women Like Me – Reclaiming Our Power

Women Like Me – Whispers of Warriors: Women Who Refused to Stay Broken

Women Like Me – Journey Through the Eyes of Kenya Women

Women Like Me Community Book Series

Women Like Me Community – Messages to My Younger Self

Women Like Me Community – Sharing Words of Gratitude

Women Like Me Community – Sharing What We Know to Be True

Women Like Me Community – Journal for Self-Discovery

Women Like Me Community – Sharing Life's Important Lessons

Women Like Me Community – Having Better Relationships

Women Like Me Community – Honoring The Women in Our Lives

Women Like Me Community – Letter's to our Future Selves